THIS BOOK IS A GIFT
OF FRIENDS
OF THE ORINDA LIBRARY

Point It Out!
TIPS FOR GREEN LIVING

The Eco-Student's Guide to Being

Green at School

by J. Angelique Johnson

illustrated by Kyle Poling

PICTURE WINDOW BOOKS
a capstone imprint

"Going green" is a hot subject in many schools. But do you know what going green really means? It means finding ways to keep our surroundings clean and healthy. These surroundings include our homes, schools, communities, and world. Going green also means learning about making healthful choices for our bodies and the bodies of others.

Check out ways you can become an eco-student by looking closely at the classrooms on the pages throughout this book.

What can we do to protect Earth?

Computer Lab Rules:

Computer Club
Join Today!

Ways to stay Green
1. Recycle
2.
3.
4.

Oh, No!
Don't throw out that pencil before it's used up! Reduce waste and sharpen it.

Way to Go!
This teacher has gone paperless to save natural resources. Ask your teacher to create a Web site. On it he can post announcements and school activities.

Way to Go!
You're using both sides of that paper. Get double-duty out of paper by writing on the blank side of handouts.

500: Science
Way to Go!
You're reducing waste by taking care of school property. Treat library books with care, and carry them in a backpack.
900: History
Oh, No!
No task lighting? Ask teachers to put in task lighting. It uses a lot less energy than overhead lighting. And it's better for your eyes.

Oh, No!

No one's in this room, but the lights are on. Ask teachers to add movement sensors to light switches in classrooms. When no one is in the room, the lights will automatically turn off.

Way to Go!

Plants clean the air naturally, making the air cleaner for you to breathe. Make sure they get plenty of water and sunlight.

Read!

Book Reports due Friday

Living Green

Book Check Out

Way to Go!

You're checking out a book. Always check your library for a book before buying it new. You'll help save the energy and resources used in making a new book.

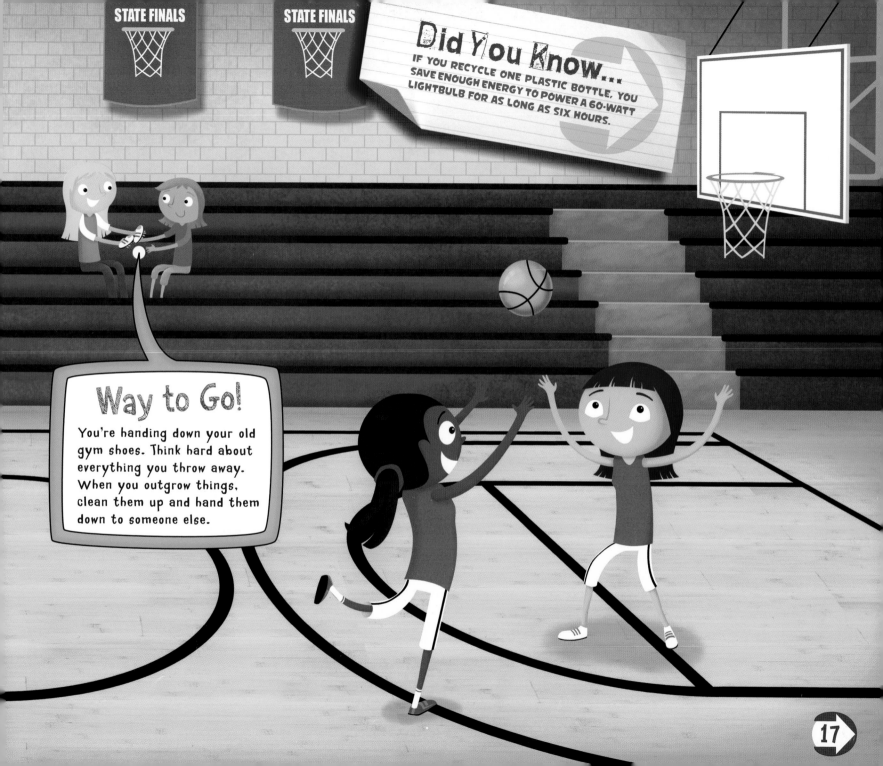

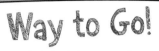

Way to Go!

That recycled toilet paper keeps the water clean. The chemicals used to bleach white toilet paper are left out. Those chemicals are bad for water.

Way to Go!

This school saves hundreds of gallons of water per day by using toilets with low gallons per flush (GPF)!

Did You Know...

MANY NEWSPAPERS, PAPER TOWELS, ALUMINUM OR GLASS CONTAINERS, STEEL CANS, AND PLASTIC LAUNDRY DETERGENT BOTTLES ARE MADE FROM RECYCLED MATERIALS. HOW COOL IS THAT?

Natural resources deserve our respect. After all, Earth provides us with food, clothing, and warmth. Unfortunately, not all resources will last forever. That means some of our resources, such as oil, can disappear if we use them up too fast. Other resources, such as water and forests, can stick around for thousands of years—but only if we take care of them.

Be an eco-student by learning all you can to help preserve Earth's resources. Look around. Do you see places where your school could make "green" improvements?

Glossary

dust jacket—a removable paper cover on a book

emissions—gases released into the air, often poisonous

Energy Star—approved by the U.S. government to save on energy use

environment—everything surrounding people, animals, and plants

landfill—land set aside where garbage is dumped and buried

natural resource—a material in nature that is useful to people

official—a person in a position of authority or trust

oxygen—a colorless gas in the air that people and animals need to live

preserve—to protect something so it stays in its original state

recycle—the process of turning something old into something new; recycling allows people to use items again; soda cans, some plastic items, newspapers, and cardboard are often recycled

reduce—to cut back on size, amount, or number

To Learn More

More Books to Read

Inches, Alison. *The Adventures of an Aluminum Can: A Story about Recycling.* Little Green Books. New York: Little Simon, 2009.

Klein, Adria F. *Max Goes to the Recycling Center.* Read-It! Readers: Red Level. Minneapolis, Minn.: Picture Window Books, 2009.

Roca, Núria. *The Three R's: Reuse, Reduce, Recycle.* What Do You Know. Hauppauge, N.Y.: Barrons Educational Series, 2007.

Internet Sites

FactHound offers a safe, fun way to find Internet sites related to this book. All of the sites on FactHound have been researched by our staff.

Here's all you do:
Visit *www.facthound.com*
Type in this code: 9781404860278

Index

Look for all of the books in the Point It Out! Tips for Green Living series:

The Eco-Family's Guide to Living Green
The Eco-Neighbor's Guide to a Green Community
The Eco-Shopper's Guide to Buying Green
The Eco-Student's Guide to Being Green at School

Special thanks to our advisers for their expertise:

Rebecca Meyer, Extension Educator
4-H Youth Development
University of Minnesota Extension, Cloquet

Terry Flaherty, PhD, Professor of English
Minnesota State University, Mankato

Editor: Shelly Lyons
Designer: Alison Thiele
Art Director: Nathan Gassman
Production Specialist: Jane Klenk

The illustrations in this book were created digitally.
Photo Credit: Shutterstock/Doodle, 22

Picture Window Books
151 Good Counsel Drive
P.O. Box 669
Mankato, MN 56002-0669
877-845-8392
www.capstonepub.com

Printed in the United States of America, North Mankato,
Minnesota. 032010 005740CGF10

All books published by Picture Window Books
are manufactured with paper containing at least
10 percent post-consumer waste.

Library of Congress Cataloging-in-Publication Data
Johnson, J. Angelique.
The eco-student's guide to being green at school /
by J. Angelique Johnson, illustrated by Kyle Poling.
    p. cm. — (Point it out! tips for green living)
  Includes index.
  ISBN 978-1-4048-6027-8 (library binding)
 1. Environmentalism—Juvenile literature. 2. Sustainable
living—Juvenile literature. 3. Green movement—Juvenile
literature.
I. Poling, Kyle, ill. II. Title.
  GE195.5.J35 2010
  640—dc22   2010010253